PRAIS.

"Terrific Icebreaker."

"Great for new friends. This game makes a terrific icebreaker
and getting-to-know-you activity."
– REAL SIMPLE MAGAZINE

"The Best You Can Find."

"If you're looking for a party game, this is the best you can find."
– THE DICE TOWER

"Simple, Easy, and Fun to Play."

"Great thought-provoking questions. Never became boring. Great
group activity for teenagers and adults. Everyone had a good time."
– iPARENTING MEDIA AWARDS

"Makes for a Lot of Laughing."

"Great family, dating, group or party game. Helps you get to know
one another better and makes for a lot of laughing. The more you
play the more creative your answers will become."
– FAMILY GAMES REVIEW

AWARDS FOR

Adding Wisdom Award, Parent to Parent

Amazing Toy Award, Parent to Parent

Creative Child Magazine Seal of Excellence

iParenting Media Award

National Association for Gifted Children Award

The National Parenting Center Seal of Approval

Award of Excellence, The Toy Man

is perfect for:

Building Friendships
Dates
Parties
Road Trips
Vacations
Icebreakers
Honeymoons
Get-Togethers
Sleepovers
Baby Showers
Birthdays
Camping
Standing in Line
Picnics
Dinner Parties
Coffee Shops
The Beach
One-on-One
or
Groups

You Can Play It Anywhere!

The Ultimate Storytelling Game

For Adults & Teens

ALLEN WOLF

MORNING STAR
PUBLISHING

You're Pulling My Leg:
the Ultimate Storytelling Game

Written by Allen Wolf, adapted from his card game

Kindly direct inquiries about this game book to:
info@MorningStarGames.com

www.AllenWolf.com
www.MorningStarGames.com

ISBN 978-1-952844-00-3

CONTENTS

THE STORY BEHIND

I originally created *You're Pulling My Leg!* as a gift for two friends who were dating, to help them get to know each other. They eventually got married! After I played the prototype game with other friends, they thought I turn it into an actual game, and I did. *You're Pulling My Leg!* has now been played by hundreds of thousands of people around the world and has won multiple awards.

You can this version of *You're Pulling My Leg!* with friends in person or over a video call. It's a great way to get to know others and forge deeper friendships. This version has questions meant for ages 13 and up.

If you'd like to play this game with younger children, I suggest *You're Pulling My Leg! Junior*. It has questions you're unlikely to know if you're part of the same household. You can still use this version, but you'll have to skip over some questions.

You're Pulling My Leg! was a staple when I was dating the woman who is now my wife! This game even appears in one of my movies.

May it bring you as much joy as it has to me. Enjoy!

All the best,

Allen Wolf
Game Creator, Filmmaker

AllenWolf.com
MorningStarGames.com

1

HOW TO PLAY

Adults & Teens • 2 or more players

Be the first to score 21 points by correctly voting on if players are telling the truth or pulling your leg and by fooling players with your own stories.

WHAT YOU'LL NEED

Coin: Use any coin or download a coin-flipping app on your phone.

Scoring Method: Use paper and pen or keep track of your score on your phone or computer. You can use the scoring pages at the back of this book to keep score as well.

STARTING THE GAME

All players start with 7 points to use for voting. Each player writes out 7 points on a piece of paper or on their phone or computer and keeps track of their own points during gameplay.

PLAYING THE GAME

1. **CHOOSE A STORYTELLER:** Choose a player to start the game as the first STORYTELLER. The Storyteller reads the three questions starting with Card 1 and announces the one they would like to answer, OR you can take turns being the Asker who chooses the question for the Storyteller to answer. If playing online, a player with the book can read the possible 3 questions out loud for the Storyteller to choose.

2. **STORYTELLER FLIPS A COIN BEFORE ANSWERING:** The Storyteller flips a coin and is the only one who sees the result. If the coin lands on HEADS, the storyteller tells a true story in response to the question. If the coin lands on TAILS, the Storyteller makes up a false story that must be untrue in essence rather than a true story with a couple of trivial facts changed.

3. **PLAYERS VOTE WITH POINTS:** After the Storyteller finishes their story, players vote points on how much they think the story is TRUE or FALSE. Players hold their fists in the air to get ready to vote while the Storyteller counts down, "One, two, three, vote!"

Players then POINT UP 1, 2, or 3 fingers if they think the story is TRUE, or POINT DOWN 1, 2, or 3 fingers if they believe the story is FALSE. Each finger represents a point, and players can vote with up to 3 fingers (3 points). Vote with 1 finger if you're not too sure or 2 or 3 if you're confident.

4. **PLAYERS WIN OR LOSE POINTS BASED ON VOTES:** The Storyteller reveals if they are telling the TRUTH or PULLING YOUR LEG. Players who voted correctly ADD the points they voted to their score. (ex: in the first round, player who voted correctly with two fingers adds 2 points to their 7 points). Players who voted incorrectly SUBTRACT what they voted from their score.

The Storyteller wins 1 point for each person they fooled, up to a MAXIMUM of 3 points per story.

5. **STORYTELLER CHOOSES NEXT STORYTELLER:** If playing in person, the person to the right of the Storyteller becomes the next Storyteller. If playing online, the Storyteller chooses the next storyteller who picks a question from the next card OR is asked a new question from the Asker. Each person should answer a question before the next round of players starts again.

If the Storyteller picks a Wild Card, the instructions must be followed BEFORE a question is answered off the card.

6. **THE FIRST PLAYER TO 21 POINTS WINS:** If playing with more than 8 people, the first person to 31 points wins or you could set a time limit. If more than one player reaches the winning points at the same time, the higher score wins. If the score is identical, the game ends in a winning tie.

PLAYING GUIDE AND TIPS

STRATEGY TIPS: The Storyteller should attempt to fool other players so they vote incorrectly and lose points. Players should keep their votes secret until everyone is ready to reveal their votes.

PASSING ON A CARD: The Storyteller may choose to advance to the next card by taking a point from their score. Before answering a new question, the Storyteller must flip the coin again. If the Storyteller has never experienced what is being asked on a card (be honest!), they can advance to the next card without giving up a point.

WILD CARDS are featured throughout the game. A Wild Card has instructions that must be followed BEFORE a question is answered from the card. If a player chooses to pass on a card (See: Passing on a Card), the Wild Card instructions must still be followed.

FALSE STORIES: False stories may have some truthful details as long as the story's essence is not true. If a player is making up a false story it does not count if the story is all true except for a few minor details. True stories need to be 100% true. If there is a disagreement, a majority vote decides the outcome.

ANSWERING STORY QUESTIONS: The Storyteller may choose whether or not to answer questions from other players about their story.

PLAYING ONLINE: When playing over a video call, the player with the game book could read the questions and have the Storyteller choose the question they would like to answer.

REPEATING A QUESTION: A Storyteller may choose to answer a question that the previous Storyteller answered.

RUNNING OUT OF POINTS: If a player runs out of points, another player may give them up to 3 points to continue the game. The player giving the points would subtract those points from their score. Otherwise, if a player runs out of points, the game ends and the player with the highest number of points wins.

RECORDING HIGHLIGHTS: If someone says something particularly funny or memorable, you can record it on the game highlight pages opposite the cards. Later you'll get a kick out of reviewing the best moments of a game.

GAME VARIATIONS

PLAYING WITH A TIMER: To speed up a game, give 1 minute to each Storyteller to begin their story, or 1 minute to tell their story. If the Storyteller does not do so by the end of their time, they lose 1 point and choose a new question.

PLAYING IN TEAMS: To play on teams, each team begins with 7 points, and each member takes turns being the Storyteller. All team members may contribute to a story, discuss whether a story is true or false, and decide their final vote.

SCORING WITH 2 PLAYERS: When playing with 2 players, if the Storyteller fools the other player, they could win the points that player voted with, rather than receiving 1 point.

VOTING ON QUESTIONS: The Storyteller could read the possible 3 questions out loud and players could vote on the question they would like to be answered.

PLAYING WITH COINS: To use coins for scoring, collect 60 pennies and 40 nickels (or any other silver coin). Each penny represents 1 point and each nickel represents 3 points. Start each player with 1 nickel and 4 pennies that represent 7 points. Place the rest of the coins into a pile for the bank. When a player votes correctly, they win the amount they voted from the bank (ex: voting 2 points gains 2). If a player votes incorrectly, they give those voting coins to the bank. A player can exchange a nickel to get 3 pennies. This is a fun way to keep score for a game.

GAME HIGHLIGHTS

When a player says something particularly funny or memorable, you can record it on a game highlights page opposite the cards. Later you'll get a kick out of reviewing the best moments of a game!

_____

_____

_____

_____

_____

_____

_____

_____

_____

_____

_____

_____

_____

_____

QUESTION CARDS

CARD 1

TELL ME ABOUT...

a new job or profession you would enjoy.

OR

something rude you have done.

OR

a time when you were the leader of something.

CARD 2

TELL ME ABOUT...

a time when you panicked about something.

OR

someone who has looked up to you.

OR

a bad experience in a restaurant.

CARD 3

TELL ME ABOUT...

one of your favorite works of art.

OR

a time when you lied to someone.

OR

a romantic situation you have experienced.

9

GAME HIGHLIGHTS

_____

_____

_____

_____

_____

_____

_____

_____

_____

_____

_____

_____

_____

_____

_____

CARD 4

TELL ME ABOUT...

someone you thought was irritating.

OR

a time when you felt threatened.

OR

a time when you arm-wrestled someone.

CARD 5

TELL ME ABOUT...

something you have cherished.

OR

a time when you accidentally cut yourself.

 Player with highest score loses 3 points; player with lowest score gains three points.

CARD 6

TELL ME ABOUT...

a favorite picture you have taken.

OR

a time when you avoided someone.

OR

something that happened when you visited your dentist.

GAME HIGHLIGHTS

_____

_____

_____

_____

_____

_____

_____

_____

_____

_____

_____

_____

_____

_____

CARD 7

TELL ME ABOUT...

a time when you had a spiritual experience.

OR

something that caused you stress.

OR

a time when you missed a deadline.

CARD 8

TELL ME ABOUT...

a time when your life changed direction.

OR

a memorable dining experience.

OR

a time when you participated in something athletic.

CARD 9

TELL ME ABOUT...

one of your favorite friends.

OR

a time when you played with a cat.

OR

a time when someone was unfriendly to you.

GAME HIGHLIGHTS

_____

_____

_____

_____

_____

_____

_____

_____

_____

_____

_____

_____

_____

_____

_____

_____

_____

CARD 10

TELL ME ABOUT...

a time when you felt alone.

OR

a time when you got muddy.

 Player with closest birthday to today gains 3 points.

CARD 11

TELL ME ABOUT...

something you would bring if you had to move to a remote island.

OR

a time when you showed affection toward someone.

OR

a time when you ate something too quickly.

CARD 12

TELL ME ABOUT...

an experience with the postal service.

OR

something you have discovered about yourself.

OR

a time when you lost something.

GAME HIGHLIGHTS

_____

_____

_____

_____

_____

_____

_____

_____

_____

_____

_____

_____

_____

_____

_____

_____

CARD 13

TELL ME ABOUT...

something about you that someone has ridiculed.

OR

something you did to try to cure yourself from a sickness.

OR

an experience watching a parade.

CARD 14

TELL ME ABOUT...

a time when you felt empty inside.

OR

one of your favorite toys from childhood.

OR

a road trip experience.

CARD 15

TELL ME ABOUT...

a time when you fought someone.

OR

a part of your body you can be uncomfortable with.

OR

a time when you did something you never thought you'd do.

GAME HIGHLIGHTS

_____

_____

_____

_____

_____

_____

_____

_____

_____

_____

_____

_____

_____

_____

CARD 16

TELL ME ABOUT...

something you have learned about yourself.

OR

a time when you saw fireworks.

 Player who exercised most recently gains 3 points.

CARD 17

TELL ME ABOUT...

a time when someone scared you.

OR

a time when you felt fulfilled.

OR

an experience at a wedding.

CARD 18

TELL ME ABOUT...

something kind you did for a stranger.

OR

a lesson you wish you had learned a while ago.

OR

a time when you danced.

GAME HIGHLIGHTS

_____

_____

_____

_____

_____

_____

_____

_____

_____

_____

_____

_____

_____

_____

CARD 19

TELL ME ABOUT...

an experience with a roommate.

OR

one of your favorite possessions.

OR

a time when a parent misunderstood you.

CARD 20

TELL ME ABOUT...

an experience wearing makeup.

OR

a time when you tried something for the first time.

OR

a time when you felt appreciated.

CARD 21

TELL ME ABOUT...

a time when you pretended to be someone else.

OR

something you would buy if you could afford it.

WILD CARD Player who got a haircut most recently loses 3 points.

GAME HIGHLIGHTS

_____

_____

_____

_____

_____

_____

_____

_____

_____

_____

_____

_____

_____

_____

_____

CARD 22

TELL ME ABOUT...

a time when you criticized someone too harshly.

OR

a situation in which you didn't feel very smart.

OR

an experience with an animal.

CARD 23

TELL ME ABOUT...

someone you have been close to.

OR

an experience at a sleepover.

OR

something about you that others would find hard to believe.

CARD 24

TELL ME ABOUT...

a game you enjoyed playing when you were a child.

OR

something a parent would do when they saw you upset.

OR

a situation in which you made a smart decision.

GAME HIGHLIGHTS

_____

_____

_____

_____

_____

_____

_____

_____

_____

_____

_____

_____

_____

_____

_____

_____

CARD 25

TELL ME ABOUT...

something that makes you feel unhealthy.

OR

something you thought would satisfy you but didn't.

OR

something you would volunteer doing full time if you could.

CARD 26

TELL ME ABOUT...

a time when you didn't want to be around anyone.

OR

someone who makes you laugh.

OR

a talent you wish you had.

CARD 27

TELL ME ABOUT...

a disease you sometimes fear getting.

OR

a misconception you have had about something.

 Player who visited a hospital most recently gains 3 points.

GAME HIGHLIGHTS

_____

_____

_____

_____

_____

_____

_____

_____

_____

_____

_____

_____

_____

_____

CARD 28

TELL ME ABOUT...

an experience with someone you thought was shallow.

OR

one of your favorite holiday memories.

OR

something you feared when you were a child.

CARD 29

TELL ME ABOUT...

an experience with someone in a wheelchair.

OR

a time when you couldn't stop laughing.

OR

something you ate too quickly.

CARD 30

TELL ME ABOUT...

a time when you felt overwhelmed.

OR

a time when you got in trouble at school or homeschool.

OR

an experience at a gym.

GAME HIGHLIGHTS

_____

_____

_____

_____

_____

_____

_____

_____

_____

_____

_____

_____

_____

_____

CARD 31

TELL ME ABOUT...

a food you used to enjoy but now do not like.

OR

a time when your bank account was almost empty.

OR

something you wish your parent(s) had done differently.

CARD 32

TELL ME ABOUT...

a time when you were inappropriately sarcastic.

OR

a time when you helped your parents when they didn't want help.

 Player who read something most recently on their phone loses 3 points.

CARD 33

TELL ME ABOUT...

someone you used to think didn't like you.

OR

someone who you think is witty.

OR

a relative who can act odd.

GAME HIGHLIGHTS

_____

_____

_____

_____

_____

_____

_____

_____

_____

_____

_____

_____

_____

_____

CARD 34

TELL ME ABOUT...

a time when you got something you didn't think you deserved.

OR

something you did that was bold.

OR

a time when you ate too much.

CARD 35

TELL ME ABOUT...

an experience at a funeral.

OR

an experience dealing with insurance.

OR

one of your favorite TV series.

CARD 36

TELL ME ABOUT...

a time when you were very sick.

OR

a time when you laughed so hard you cried.

OR

something you got caught doing.

31

GAME HIGHLIGHTS

_____

_____

_____

_____

_____

_____

_____

_____

_____

_____

_____

_____

_____

_____

CARD 37

TELL ME ABOUT...

a friend you wish you hadn't lost in touch with.

OR

a time when you were a bad influence on someone.

OR

a time in your life when you overcame something.

CARD 38

TELL ME ABOUT...

a time when you got revenge for something.

OR

a time when you stepped on gum.

 Youngest player loses 3 points. Oldest player gains 3 points.

CARD 39

TELL ME ABOUT...

Something you used to wear that you wish you still could.

OR

a time when you felt defeated.

OR

an experience listening to music.

33

GAME HIGHLIGHTS

CARD 40

TELL ME ABOUT...

something you have cheered for.

OR

a time when you lacked self-control.

OR

something that disgusted you.

CARD 41

TELL ME ABOUT...

someone you admired when you were a child.

OR

a time when you thought you would be punished but weren't.

OR

something in your life you want to be different in five years.

CARD 42

TELL ME ABOUT...

an accomplishment you are proud of.

OR

someone you have envied.

OR

a time when you did something challenging.

GAME HIGHLIGHTS

_____

_____

_____

_____

_____

_____

_____

_____

_____

_____

_____

_____

_____

_____

_____

CARD 43

TELL ME ABOUT...

a time when you got revenge for something.

OR

a time in your life you would repeat if you could.

WILD CARD Storyteller chooses a player who loses 3 points.

CARD 44

TELL ME ABOUT...

a time when you thought your life might end.

OR

a time when you felt foolish.

OR

a time when you binge-watched something.

CARD 45

TELL ME ABOUT...

an animal you would be if you could.

OR

something you have failed at doing.

OR

a friend who seems to have an easy life.

GAME HIGHLIGHTS

_____

_____

_____

_____

_____

_____

_____

_____

_____

_____

_____

_____

_____

_____

_____

CARD 46

TELL ME ABOUT...

someone you would switch places with if you could.

OR

someone from your past you thought would eventually succeed.

OR

a time when you lost your temper.

CARD 47

TELL ME ABOUT...

one of your favorite foods.

OR

a mistake you made while working on something.

OR

a time when your expectations of yourself were too high.

CARD 48

TELL ME ABOUT...

something you regret from your past.

OR

a place you would like to go that feels peaceful.

OR

something you didn't do because you were afraid.

GAME HIGHLIGHTS

_____

_____

_____

_____

_____

_____

_____

_____

_____

_____

_____

_____

_____

_____

_____

CARD 49

TELL ME ABOUT...

a time when you overspent.

OR

someone you have a hard time liking.

WILD CARD Player with longest hair gains 3 points.

CARD 50

TELL ME ABOUT...

a time when you experienced something miraculous.

OR

something that was stolen from you.

OR

a time when you believed bad medical advice.

CARD 51

TELL ME ABOUT...

one of your favorite teachers or speakers.

OR

a time when you experienced something about God.

OR

someone you know who is shy.

GAME HIGHLIGHTS

_____

_____

_____

_____

_____

_____

_____

_____

_____

_____

_____

_____

_____

CARD 52

TELL ME ABOUT...

a child you thought was annoying.

OR

a time when you broke a promise to a friend.

OR

a time when you felt obligated to do something.

CARD 53

TELL ME ABOUT...

someone to whom you were once attracted.

OR

something that refreshes you.

OR

something others can do that makes you feel special.

CARD 54

TELL ME ABOUT...

someone who has had a positive impact on your life.

OR

a time when you forgot to do something.

 Players who have any red in their clothing lose 3 points.

GAME HIGHLIGHTS

CARD 55

TELL ME ABOUT...

a time when you didn't feel loved.

OR

an instrument you have played or wish you could play.

OR

a time when your phone died.

CARD 56

TELL ME ABOUT...

someone you know who is overly optimistic.

OR

a time when you yelled at something you were watching.

OR

a time when you thought you might suffocate.

CARD 57

TELL ME ABOUT...

something you look forward to.

OR

an experience at a picnic.

OR

a way you like to show affection.

GAME HIGHLIGHTS

_____

_____

_____

_____

_____

_____

_____

_____

_____

_____

_____

_____

_____

_____

CARD 58

TELL ME ABOUT...

something you would do if it wasn't illegal.

OR

an experience coloring or drawing a picture.

OR

a good memory about your grandparent(s).

CARD 59

TELL ME ABOUT...

a possession that gives you comfort.

OR

a time when someone fooled you.

OR

a time when you felt exhausted.

CARD 60

TELL ME ABOUT...

a car you would like to own.

OR

something that excites you.

WILD CARD   Player with lowest score gains 3 points.

GAME HIGHLIGHTS

CARD 61

TELL ME ABOUT...

something you have felt guilty about.

OR

a time when you were mistaken for someone else.

OR

an experience carving something.

CARD 62

TELL ME ABOUT...

a time when you felt helpless.

OR

something you found.

OR

a time when you felt like someone was staring at you.

CARD 63

TELL ME ABOUT...

an experience that humbled you.

OR

a time when you stole something.

OR

a time when you worried about your parent(s).

GAME HIGHLIGHTS

_____

_____

_____

_____

_____

_____

_____

_____

_____

_____

_____

_____

_____

CARD 64

TELL ME ABOUT...

an ad you saw that you liked.

OR

a part of your personality you would change if you could.

OR

an experience at a surprise party.

CARD 65

TELL ME ABOUT...

something you felt provoked to do.

OR

a time when you felt cheated.

 Player who grew up farthest away gains 3 points.

CARD 66

TELL ME ABOUT...

someone you know who is stubborn.

OR

a time when you were proved innocent of something.

OR

someone you wish you could be related to.

GAME HIGHLIGHTS

CARD 67

TELL ME ABOUT...

one of your favorite pieces of clothing.

OR

something you would achieve if nothing was holding you back.

OR

something you'd do differently if given another chance.

CARD 68

TELL ME ABOUT...

something that has made you angry.

OR

a time when your parents yelled at you.

OR

something you wish you could change about your work.

CARD 69

TELL ME ABOUT...

a time when you didn't sleep well.

OR

a time when a relative did something funny.

OR

a time when someone took advantage of your kindness.

GAME HIGHLIGHTS

_____

_____

_____

_____

_____

_____

_____

_____

_____

_____

_____

_____

_____

_____

_____

_____

_____

CARD 70

TELL ME ABOUT...

something about your family you wish was different.

OR

a relationship that was difficult for you.

OR

a childhood friend.

CARD 71

TELL ME ABOUT...

a time when you stayed up very late.

OR

an experience with God.

 Player who swam most recently gains 3 points.

CARD 72

TELL ME ABOUT...

a day when everything went right.

OR

something you can be sensitive about.

OR

an awkward conversation you had with someone.

GAME HIGHLIGHTS

_____

_____

_____

_____

_____

_____

_____

_____

_____

_____

_____

_____

_____

_____

CARD 73

TELL ME ABOUT...

something you found inside a couch.

OR

something that is unresolved between you and someone else.

OR

how you feel about one of your friendships.

CARD 74

TELL ME ABOUT...

something unfortunate that happened to you.

OR

a habit you have tried to break.

OR

a time when something surprising happened.

CARD 75

TELL ME ABOUT...

something few people know about you.

OR

something you have a hard time refusing.

OR

one of your favorite fruits.

GAME HIGHLIGHTS

_____

_____

_____

_____

_____

_____

_____

_____

_____

_____

_____

_____

_____

_____

CARD 76

TELL ME ABOUT...

a compliment someone gave you.

OR

something mischievous you have done.

 Player who attended a wedding most recently gains 3 points.

CARD 77

TELL ME ABOUT...

a time when a friend surprised you with something.

OR

a time when you took a risk.

OR

someone you think has acted strangely.

CARD 78

TELL ME ABOUT...

something that has made you cry.

OR

something you find attractive in others.

OR

a time when you wished you had treated your parent(s) differently.

GAME HIGHLIGHTS

_____

_____

_____

_____

_____

_____

_____

_____

_____

_____

_____

_____

_____

_____

_____

CARD 79

TELL ME ABOUT...

someone who has hurt you.

OR

something you learned about life from a parent.

OR

anywhere in the world you would live if you could.

CARD 80

TELL ME ABOUT...

something you have done that was daring.

OR

something you can be insecure about.

OR

a toy you broke or lost when you were a child.

CARD 81

TELL ME ABOUT...

a low point in your life that changed you.

OR

a time when you had a cold or the flu.

OR

something you prayed for that you're thankful didn't happen.

GAME HIGHLIGHTS

_____

_____

_____

_____

_____

_____

_____

_____

_____

_____

_____

_____

_____

_____

CARD 82

TELL ME ABOUT...

something you worked hard to earn.

OR

a mishap when you were a student.

 Player who did laundry most recently gains 3 points.

CARD 83

TELL ME ABOUT...

something you don't like others doing.

OR

a time in your life when you were extremely happy.

OR

someone you think is opinionated.

CARD 84

TELL ME ABOUT...

a time when someone was too nosy.

OR

a time when you or someone you knew was in a car accident.

OR

a friend you wish you could spend more time with.

GAME HIGHLIGHTS

CARD 85

TELL ME ABOUT...

a place where you used to buy groceries.

OR

something that happened last year that was unexpected.

OR

someone you had a crush on when you were a child.

CARD 86

TELL ME ABOUT...

an experience that was traumatic for you.

OR

one of your favorite songs.

OR

something you have frequently bought.

CARD 87

TELL ME ABOUT...

something you remember about your first job.

OR

a time when you got in trouble for something.

WILD CARD Oldest player loses 3 points. Youngest player gains three points.

GAME HIGHLIGHTS

_____

_____

_____

_____

_____

_____

_____

_____

_____

_____

_____

_____

_____

_____

_____

_____

CARD 88

TELL ME ABOUT...

a fun vacation experience.

OR

one of your favorite vegetables.

OR

something that interests your parent(s).

CARD 89

TELL ME ABOUT...

someone you know who talks too much.

OR

a time when you were rewarded for something.

OR

a time when you were amazed by something.

CARD 90

TELL ME ABOUT...

something disappointing that has happened in a job or your career.

OR

a time when you asked someone for forgiveness.

OR

an experience inside a tunnel.

GAME HIGHLIGHTS

_____

_____

_____

_____

_____

_____

_____

_____

_____

_____

_____

_____

_____

_____

_____

_____

_____

CARD 91

TELL ME ABOUT...

a time when everything looked hopeless but turned out all right.

OR

an ex-boyfriend or girlfriend.

OR

something that has medically gone wrong with you.

CARD 92

TELL ME ABOUT...

a part of the world you like the most.

OR

a topic of conversation your family avoided.

OR

a time when you misjudged someone.

CARD 93

TELL ME ABOUT...

a successful person you don't think should have that much success.

OR

one of your favorite movies.

WILD CARD Player who sang most recently gains 3 points.

GAME HIGHLIGHTS

CARD 94

TELL ME ABOUT...

someone who was difficult for you to forgive.

OR

an emotion that can be difficult for you to express.

OR

something you did that was artistic.

CARD 95

TELL ME ABOUT...

a bad vacation experience.

OR

one of your first dating experiences.

OR

a time when someone misjudged you.

CARD 96

TELL ME ABOUT...

one of your favorite books.

OR

one of your favorite dreams.

OR

Something you look forward to that will happen next week.

GAME HIGHLIGHTS

_____

_____

_____

_____

_____

_____

_____

_____

_____

_____

_____

_____

_____

_____

CARD 97

TELL ME ABOUT...

a time when you felt overworked.

OR

a time when something unusual happened to you.

OR

one of your favorite ice cream flavors.

CARD 98

TELL ME ABOUT...

something you used to enjoy doing with a group of friends.

OR

one of your favorite soups.

 Storyteller chooses another player who gains 3 points.

CARD 99

TELL ME ABOUT...

a characteristic of a sibling.

OR

a favorite pet you once owned.

OR

a time when you got hurt while playing a sport.

GAME HIGHLIGHTS

_____

_____

_____

_____

_____

_____

_____

_____

_____

_____

_____

_____

_____

CARD 100

TELL ME ABOUT...

an experience getting your hair cut.

OR

an experience recycling.

OR

something you would change about your looks if you could.

CARD 101

TELL ME ABOUT...

someone you admire.

OR

something you got away with as a kid.

OR

something you have enjoyed learning.

CARD 102

TELL ME ABOUT...

one of your favorite classes.

OR

someone you wish would like you better.

OR

one of your favorite TV shows when you were a child.

GAME HIGHLIGHTS

CARD 103

TELL ME ABOUT...

a luxury you would enjoy having.

OR

something you did that made your parent(s) mad.

OR

a dating experience when you were a student.

CARD 104

TELL ME ABOUT...

one of the purposes of your life.

OR

an experience involving the police.

 Player who saw a movie most recently gains 3 points.

CARD 105

TELL ME ABOUT...

something you have done to improve your health.

OR

one of your favorite snacks.

OR

a time when you felt like you had a lot of power.

GAME HIGHLIGHTS

_____

_____

_____

_____

_____

_____

_____

_____

_____

_____

_____

_____

_____

_____

_____

CARD 106

TELL ME ABOUT...

someone from your childhood who was a bully.

OR

something you often did with friends while growing up.

OR

one of the professions you aspired to as a child.

CARD 107

TELL ME ABOUT...

how your parent(s) treated you when you did something wrong.

OR

someone you did not get along with.

OR

one of your dream houses.

CARD 108

TELL ME ABOUT...

a name you wouldn't mind changing your name to.

OR

a part of your body that sometimes hurts.

OR

something you hope will happen in the next 10 years.

GAME HIGHLIGHTS

CARD 109

TELL ME ABOUT...

someone you used to be infatuated with.

OR

a time when an insect or rodent frightened you.

 Player with lowest score switches point scores with player of their choice.

CARD 110

TELL ME ABOUT...

a time in your life when you overcame something.

OR

a time when something got stuck in your hair.

OR

a time when you were on the phone for a really long time.

CARD 111

TELL ME ABOUT...

a time when you helped someone.

OR

a time when you used bad language.

OR

a time when you were talking to a friend and the friend cried.

GAME HIGHLIGHTS

_____

_____

_____

_____

_____

_____

_____

_____

_____

_____

_____

_____

_____

CARD 112

TELL ME ABOUT...

something you would like to do after you retire.

OR

a time when you realized you were being insensitive.

OR

something about yourself that can be hard for you to accept.

CARD 113

TELL ME ABOUT...

someone you once bullied around.

OR

an experience star-gazing.

OR

a time when you faked being sick.

CARD 114

TELL ME ABOUT...

a time when you were the center of attention.

OR

a time when you hurt someone unintentionally.

OR

a time when you were passionate about voting for something.

GAME HIGHLIGHTS

CARD 115

TELL ME ABOUT...

a favorite stuffed animal from your childhood.

OR

something you have feared.

 Player who finished a book most recently gains 3 points.

CARD 116

TELL ME ABOUT...

something you were known for when you were a child.

OR

one of the oldest people you know.

OR

a cartoon character you would be if you could.

CARD 117

TELL ME ABOUT...

a memory you would like to remember 20 years from now.

OR

a time when someone forgave you.

OR

a good memory involving a pet.

GAME HIGHLIGHTS

_____

_____

_____

_____

_____

_____

_____

_____

_____

_____

_____

_____

_____

_____

CARD 118

TELL ME ABOUT...

one of your favorite amusement park rides.

OR

a magic trick you have performed.

OR

a time when you were a supportive friend to someone.

CARD 119

TELL ME ABOUT...

something you have done that was childlike.

OR

a time when there was too much pressure on you.

OR

something you overheard someone saying.

CARD 120

TELL ME ABOUT...

a time when you hid something and it was found.

OR

a time when something didn't go your way.

WILD CARD Storyteller chooses a player who loses 3 points.

GAME HIGHLIGHTS

_____

_____

_____

_____

_____

_____

_____

_____

_____

_____

_____

_____

CARD 121

TELL ME ABOUT...

one of your favorite places to eat.

OR

something you wish would've happened differently last year.

OR

an embarrassing moment.

CARD 122

TELL ME ABOUT...

an experience in bad weather.

OR

a time when someone didn't believe you even though you were telling the truth.

OR

an experience you have had in water.

CARD 123

TELL ME ABOUT...

a favorite place to play when you were a child.

OR

a time when someone else took credit for something you did.

OR

a contest you won.

GAME HIGHLIGHTS

_____

_____

_____

_____

_____

_____

_____

_____

_____

_____

_____

_____

_____

_____

_____

CARD 124

TELL ME ABOUT...

a prayer you prayed that was answered.

OR

a time when you thought your life was in danger.

OR

one of your favorite sports teams.

CARD 125

TELL ME ABOUT...

a favorite superhero.

OR

one of the ways you think your life might end.

OR

another family you wished to be a part of when you were a child.

CARD 126

TELL ME ABOUT...

a time when you were very cold.

OR

something you used to avoid doing.

WILD CARD Player who saw a play most recently gains 3 points.

GAME HIGHLIGHTS

_____

_____

_____

_____

_____

_____

_____

_____

_____

_____

_____

_____

_____

_____

_____

_____

CARD 127

TELL ME ABOUT...

something adventurous you did with you parent(s).

OR

a time when you kept a promise even though it was difficult.

OR

a time when you visited a zoo.

CARD 128

TELL ME ABOUT...

a time when you did something political.

OR

one of your favorite places to eat in your hometown.

OR

an experience with someone from another country.

CARD 129

TELL ME ABOUT...

someone you have gone to for advice.

OR

a date that didn't go well.

OR

an experience with an email or text.

GAME HIGHLIGHTS

_____

_____

_____

_____

_____

_____

_____

_____

_____

_____

_____

_____

_____

_____

CARD 130

TELL ME ABOUT...

a time when you stood up for something.

OR

a time when someone corrected you when you were wrong.

OR

a scary dream.

CARD 131

TELL ME ABOUT...

a time when you got up very early.

OR

something you have constructed.

 Player with shortest last name loses 3 points.

CARD 132

TELL ME ABOUT...

a memory of watching sports when you were a child.

OR

an experience cooking.

OR

a time when you felt betrayed.

GAME HIGHLIGHTS

_____

_____

_____

_____

_____

_____

_____

_____

_____

_____

_____

_____

_____

_____

_____

CARD 133

TELL ME ABOUT...

one of the rules in your family when you were a child.

OR

a favorite concert or musical.

OR

one of your good habits.

CARD 134

TELL ME ABOUT...

something you have destroyed.

OR

a movie ending you didn't like.

OR

a time when you ate a lot of candy.

CARD 135

TELL ME ABOUT...

a time when you sneaked into something.

OR

a time when you discovered something shocking.

OR

a situation in which you were dressed inappropriately.

GAME HIGHLIGHTS

_____

_____

_____

_____

_____

_____

_____

_____

_____

_____

_____

_____

_____

_____

CARD 136

TELL ME ABOUT...

one of your favorite items to order at a fast food restaurant.

OR

a time when you fell in love with someone or something.

OR

a time when you began to look at something differently.

CARD 137

TELL ME ABOUT...

a time when you were suspicious about something.

OR

an experience skating.

 Player who woke up earliest today gains 3 points.

CARD 138

TELL ME ABOUT...

a time when you got some great news.

OR

a time when you thought about running away.

OR

something interesting you have done.

GAME HIGHLIGHTS

_____

_____

_____

_____

_____

_____

_____

_____

_____

_____

_____

_____

_____

CARD 139

TELL ME ABOUT...

a role you would have played if you were an actor.

OR

gossip that was said about you.

OR

a place you would be scared to visit.

CARD 140

TELL ME ABOUT...

a time when you felt like you were not in control.

OR

something you once believed but no longer do.

OR

a costume you have worn.

CARD 141

TELL ME ABOUT...

a magic trick you have performed.

OR

a time when you ate too much candy.

OR

something you were wrong about.

GAME HIGHLIGHTS

_____

_____

_____

_____

_____

_____

_____

_____

_____

_____

_____

_____

_____

_____

CARD 142

TELL ME ABOUT...

an experience using a navigation system.

OR

a time when you felt loved.

OR

a beautiful sunset you remember.

CARD 143

TELL ME ABOUT...

something that has upset you.

OR

a time when you sang.

 Players wearing white socks lose 3 points.

CARD 144

TELL ME ABOUT...

something regretful that happened at work.

OR

a way you showed compassion to someone.

OR

something you learned from a movie or TV.

GAME HIGHLIGHTS

_____

_____

_____

_____

_____

_____

_____

_____

_____

_____

_____

_____

_____

_____

CARD 145

TELL ME ABOUT...

someone who has gotten on your nerves.

OR

a time when you were suspicious of something.

OR

something about yourself you sometimes compare to others.

CARD 146

TELL ME ABOUT...

something socially awkward you have done.

OR

a time when you were irresponsible with money.

OR

an experience riding a bike.

CARD 147

TELL ME ABOUT...

a fancy dinner you enjoyed.

OR

an example of how your parents treated each other.

OR

an experience buying music.

GAME HIGHLIGHTS

CARD 148

TELL ME ABOUT...

something you like about someone from another country.

OR

someone who has come through for you in a difficult time.

OR

a realization you had after spending time by yourself.

CARD 149

TELL ME ABOUT...

one of your favorite places to spend time.

OR

a time when you traveled in an airplane.

WILD CARD Player who has the most pets gains 3 points.

CARD 150

TELL ME ABOUT...

an opportunity you once had but lost.

OR

something you did when someone got angry at you.

OR

a time when you felt insulted.

GAME HIGHLIGHTS

CARD 151

TELL ME ABOUT...

an experience with an emergency.

OR

one of your earliest memories.

OR

something you wish your parent(s) did more.

CARD 152

TELL ME ABOUT...

one of your favorite wintertime activities when you were a child.

OR

how you are similar to one of your relatives.

OR

someone you liked who did not like you.

CARD 153

TELL ME ABOUT...

something you would change about the government.

OR

an experience on a boat.

OR

something you like to do indoors.

GAME HIGHLIGHTS

CARD 154

TELL ME ABOUT...

one of your close friends from school.

OR

something you have always wanted to do.

 Player who traveled to another city most recently gains 3 points.

CARD 155

TELL ME ABOUT...

a party you enjoyed.

OR

feedback about yourself that you disagreed with.

OR

something you would erase from your memory if you could.

CARD 156

TELL ME ABOUT...

something you have done that was dangerous.

OR

a family holiday tradition.

OR

how you would change someone you know.

GAME HIGHLIGHTS

_____

_____

_____

_____

_____

_____

_____

_____

_____

_____

_____

_____

_____

_____

_____

CARD 157

TELL ME ABOUT...

a challenge you have faced.

OR

a friend you think is interesting.

OR

something that has motivated you.

CARD 158

TELL ME ABOUT...

an important decision you had to make.

OR

something you have refused to eat.

OR

something you have taken for granted.

CARD 159

TELL ME ABOUT...

an experience celebrating your birthday.

OR

something you have worried about.

OR

something you wish was different about your childhood.

GAME HIGHLIGHTS

_____

_____

_____

_____

_____

_____

_____

_____

_____

_____

_____

_____

_____

_____

CARD 160

TELL ME ABOUT...

an experience at an amusement park.

OR

something you often did with your family while growing up.

WILD CARD Player with the most freckles gains 3 points.

CARD 161

TELL ME ABOUT...

a time when you got into debt.

OR

something you did for someone you were in love with.

OR

an experience at an airport.

CARD 162

TELL ME ABOUT...

a time when you saw someone you hadn't seen for a long time.

OR

one of your favorite podcasts.

OR

something memorable you have seen.

GAME HIGHLIGHTS

CARD 163

TELL ME ABOUT...

someone who has religious beliefs you do not agree with.

OR

one of the longest conversations you have had.

OR

an experience in school gym class or playing sports.

CARD 164

TELL ME ABOUT...

a favorite hobby.

OR

a time when someone confronted you about something.

OR

an experience that happened late at night.

CARD 165

TELL ME ABOUT...

someone you helped who was disadvantaged.

OR

something you would like to accomplish before you die.

WILD CARD Players wearing jeans lose 3 points.

GAME HIGHLIGHTS

CARD 166

TELL ME ABOUT...

an experience paying taxes.

OR

a previous nickname.

OR

someone you know who is a good listener.

CARD 167

TELL ME ABOUT...

a fictional character you would be if you could.

OR

something gross you have eaten.

OR

a time when you decorated something.

CARD 168

TELL ME ABOUT...

a time when you eavesdropped on a conversation.

OR

an experience in the rain.

OR

a time when you quit something.

GAME HIGHLIGHTS

_____

_____

_____

_____

_____

_____

_____

_____

_____

_____

_____

_____

_____

CARD 169

TELL ME ABOUT...

a time when you felt popular.

OR

something you predicted that came true.

OR

an experience at a hospital.

CARD 170

TELL ME ABOUT...

an experience on a train.

OR

something you would do if you had only 30 more days to live.

OR

one of your favorite colors.

CARD 171

TELL ME ABOUT...

an experience in a cafeteria.

OR

something you spent your allowance on while growing up.

WILD CARD Storyteller switches their score with any player.

GAME HIGHLIGHTS

_____

_____

_____

_____

_____

_____

_____

_____

_____

_____

_____

_____

_____

_____

CARD 172

TELL ME ABOUT...

something you persuaded someone else to do.

OR

an experience camping.

OR

something you remember from kindergarten.

CARD 173

TELL ME ABOUT...

something your family did on weekends during your childhood.

OR

an experience at a museum.

OR

a time when you raced someone.

CARD 174

TELL ME ABOUT...

a compliment that can be difficult for you to receive.

OR

something you filmed yourself doing but later regretted.

OR

an experience playing a video game.

GAME HIGHLIGHTS

_____

_____

_____

_____

_____

_____

_____

_____

_____

_____

_____

_____

_____

_____

CARD 175

TELL ME ABOUT...

something you like to do during the summer.

OR

an experience in a toy store.

OR

something that scared you in the middle of the night.

CARD 176

TELL ME ABOUT...

an experience helping an animal.

OR

a news event that impacted you.

 Player with the most colors in their clothing gains 3 points.

CARD 177

TELL ME ABOUT...

a possession you would save if your home was on fire.

OR

an experience with a lawyer.

OR

something healthy you like to eat.

GAME HIGHLIGHTS

_____

_____

_____

_____

_____

_____

_____

_____

_____

_____

_____

_____

_____

_____

_____

CARD 178

TELL ME ABOUT...

one of the best gifts someone has given to you.

OR

someone you didn't like until you got to know them better.

OR

an experience with someone much older than you.

CARD 179

TELL ME ABOUT...

a gift you returned or wish you returned.

OR

one of your favorite beverages.

OR

a subject you excelled at in school.

CARD 180

TELL ME ABOUT...

a friend's pet you didn't like.

OR

something that happened in your neighborhood during your youth.

OR

a friend your parents did not like you having.

GAME HIGHLIGHTS

_____

_____

_____

_____

_____

_____

_____

_____

_____

_____

_____

_____

_____

CARD 181

TELL ME ABOUT...

a time when you trained for something.

OR

an experience with a cell phone.

OR

something about your hometown.

CARD 182

TELL ME ABOUT...

an opinion you have that some people don't agree with.

OR

something you have been passionate about.

WILD CARD Player who went online most recently gains 3 points.

CARD 183

TELL ME ABOUT...

an experience working on a car.

OR

an argument you had with someone.

OR

an experience watching the Olympics.

GAME HIGHLIGHTS

_____

_____

_____

_____

_____

_____

_____

_____

_____

_____

_____

_____

_____

_____

CARD 184

TELL ME ABOUT...

a time when you regretted posting something online.

OR

someone you know who ran away or went missing for a time.

OR

what you thought you would be like as an adult.

CARD 185

TELL ME ABOUT...

someone you know who acts lazy.

OR

something you would do if it was not immoral.

OR

one of your favorite sandwiches.

CARD 186

TELL ME ABOUT...

an experience with a baby.

OR

a time when you cut your own hair.

OR

a day when everything went wrong.

GAME HIGHLIGHTS

CARD 187

TELL ME ABOUT...

a celebrity you admire.

OR

something you like about the outdoors.

 Player with longest last name gains 3 points.

CARD 188

TELL ME ABOUT...

something you have prioritized.

OR

an experience at a circus.

OR

a superhero power you would like to have.

CARD 189

TELL ME ABOUT...

one of your favorite cereals from your childhood.

OR

something creative you have done.

OR

one of your former bosses.

GAME HIGHLIGHTS

_____

_____

_____

_____

_____

_____

_____

_____

_____

_____

_____

_____

_____

_____

CARD 190

TELL ME ABOUT...

something you remember from when you turned 13 years old.

OR

something you've done when no one else was around.

OR

one of the ways you are different from your parent(s).

CARD 191

TELL ME ABOUT...

someone you wish you had a closer relationship with.

OR

something important your parent(s) taught you.

OR

a time when you were gullible about something.

CARD 192

TELL ME ABOUT...

an experience riding a bus.

OR

a similarity between you and one of your parents.

OR

one of your favorite flowers.

GAME HIGHLIGHTS

_____

_____

_____

_____

_____

_____

_____

_____

_____

_____

_____

_____

_____

_____

_____

_____

CARD 193

TELL ME ABOUT...

an experience during a hot day.

OR

something you believe is important to bring when traveling.

WILD CARD Shortest player gains 3 points.

CARD 194

TELL ME ABOUT...

an awkward dating experience.

OR

an experience at a library.

OR

a time when you were generous.

CARD 195

TELL ME ABOUT...

a fun experience with your parent(s).

OR

someone you were concerned about when you were a student.

OR

an experience at a doctor's office.

GAME HIGHLIGHTS

_____

_____

_____

_____

_____

_____

_____

_____

_____

_____

_____

_____

_____

_____

CARD 196

TELL ME ABOUT...

an experience swimming.

OR

a time when you slipped on something.

OR

one of your favorite moments in sports.

CARD 197

TELL ME ABOUT...

someone you have dated.

OR

something you have dreamed about.

OR

a time when you woke up in the middle of the night.

CARD 198

TELL ME ABOUT...

a time when you should have confronted someone but didn't.

OR

a time when you wish you could have been in two places at once.

WILD CARD Player who rode a bike most recently gains 3 points.

GAME HIGHLIGHTS

CARD 199

TELL ME ABOUT...

a compliment you gave someone.

OR

one of your weaknesses.

OR

a time when something in your life seemed unmanageable.

CARD 200

TELL ME ABOUT...

a characteristic of a grandparent.

OR

a time when you felt depressed.

OR

a singer you would switch places with if you could.

CARD 201

TELL ME ABOUT...

something you have collected.

OR

someone you think is intimidating.

OR

something you have recovered from.

GAME HIGHLIGHTS

_____

_____

_____

_____

_____

_____

_____

_____

_____

_____

_____

_____

_____

_____

_____

CARD 202

TELL ME ABOUT...

a time when you witnessed racism.

OR

something interesting you found online.

OR

a moment when you spent too much time doing something.

CARD 203

TELL ME ABOUT...

an experience using a credit card.

OR

a favorite place your family liked to go for vacation.

OR

a time when you thought you were better than someone else.

CARD 204

TELL ME ABOUT...

a time when you counseled a friend.

OR

something of yours that someone damaged or broke.

WILD CARD Player with highest score loses 3 points.

GAME HIGHLIGHTS

_____

_____

_____

_____

_____

_____

_____

_____

_____

_____

_____

_____

_____

_____

CARD 205

TELL ME ABOUT...

a time when you were bored.

OR

a time when your parent(s) avoided you.

OR

a dream that gave you insight.

CARD 206

TELL ME ABOUT...

something a close friend did that hurt you.

OR

a time when you got a speeding ticket.

OR

an experience with laundry.

CARD 207

TELL ME ABOUT...

an experience with the Bible.

OR

something you did that was patriotic.

OR

a time in your life when your values changed.

GAME HIGHLIGHTS

CARD 208

TELL ME ABOUT...

one of your favorite smells.

OR

a time when your car ran out of gas.

OR

an injustice that happened to you or a friend.

CARD 209

TELL ME ABOUT...

a time when you noticed that someone had gotten older.

OR

a family tradition.

 Players wearing athletic shoes lose 3 points.

CARD 210

TELL ME ABOUT...

something you have broken.

OR

a time when you didn't listen to someone in authority.

OR

what someone told you that you later discovered wasn't true.

GAME HIGHLIGHTS

_____

_____

_____

_____

_____

_____

_____

_____

_____

_____

_____

_____

_____

_____

_____

CARD 211

TELL ME ABOUT...

an experience driving.

OR

a club or organization of which you were a member.

OR

a time when you almost gave up on something.

CARD 212

TELL ME ABOUT...

a time when you watched something live.

OR

one of your favorite games (other than this one).

OR

an experience with a pet.

CARD 213

TELL ME ABOUT...

an experience with junk food.

OR

something you have asked your grandparent(s).

OR

a chore you did during your youth.

GAME HIGHLIGHTS

_____

_____

_____

_____

_____

_____

_____

_____

_____

_____

_____

_____

_____

CARD 214

TELL ME ABOUT...

someone who has given you a compliment.

OR

something painful you have stepped on.

OR

a time when you tried something new.

CARD 215

TELL ME ABOUT...

an embarrassing situation involving an odor.

OR

a time when you saw a dead animal or insect.

 Player who gave a compliment most recently gains 3 points.

CARD 216

TELL ME ABOUT...

someone you know who was impacted by a divorce.

OR

an experience with a computer.

OR

one of your favorite places to eat breakfast or lunch.

GAME HIGHLIGHTS

CARD 217

TELL ME ABOUT...

a phone conversation that upset you.

OR

an experience with plants or flowers.

OR

a time when you took a tour of something.

CARD 218

TELL ME ABOUT...

one of your closest friends.

OR

something you wish someone had been recognized for.

OR

an experience on a lake.

CARD 219

TELL ME ABOUT...

a time when you gave someone a thoughtful present.

OR

an experience with a loud person.

OR

a time when you discovered your zipper was down.

GAME HIGHLIGHTS

_____

_____

_____

_____

_____

_____

_____

_____

_____

_____

_____

_____

_____

_____

CARD 220

TELL ME ABOUT...

something you would like to be different in the world in 100 years.

OR

a time when you were extremely late for something.

 Player with the most scars gains 3 points.

CARD 221

TELL ME ABOUT...

something you like to do to relax.

OR

an experience at a bakery.

OR

a time when you defended someone.

CARD 222

TELL ME ABOUT...

a time when you went too long before getting a haircut.

OR

something you did that was silly.

OR

a different period of time you would visit if you could.

GAME HIGHLIGHTS

_____

_____

_____

_____

_____

_____

_____

_____

_____

_____

_____

_____

_____

_____

_____

_____

CARD 223

TELL ME ABOUT...

a time when you felt sorry for someone.

OR

a time when you were jealous.

OR

a time when someone treated you better than you deserved.

CARD 224

TELL ME ABOUT...

a favorite documentary.

OR

a favorite perfume or cologne.

OR

something you became obsessed with.

CARD 225

TELL ME ABOUT...

a time when you fell off of something.

OR

a time when you threw a snowball.

OR

a time when you saw a magic trick.

ABOUT THE GAME CREATOR

Allen Wolf has won multiple accolades for creating games, movies, and novels. He has won 38 awards for the games he has created that include *You're Pulling My Leg!*, *You're Pulling My Leg! Junior*, *Slap Wacky*, *JabberJot*, and *Pet Detectives*. These games have brought smiles to hundreds of thousands of people around the world.

Allen is also a movie writer, director, and producer. *You're Pulling My Leg!* appears in his novel *Hooked*, that is now a major motion picture.

You're Pulling My Leg! also makes a prominent appearance in Allen's first feature film, *In My Sleep*, that was released worldwide and won multiple film festival awards.

Allen graduated from New York University's film school, where his senior thesis film, *Harlem Grace*, won multiple festival awards and was a finalist for the *Student Academy Awards*.

Allen married his Persian princess, and they are raising their daughter and son. He enjoys traveling around the world and hearing people's life stories. He also cherishes playing games with his family, tasting chocolate, and visiting Disneyland, where he has been over 500 times.

Connect with Allen:

AllenWolf.com
MorningStarGames.com

 @theAllenWolf

 @theAllenWolf

 @theAllenWolf

OTHER GAMES FROM ALLEN WOLF

Have you ever eaten five pizzas? Gotten gum stuck in your hair? Surprised a friend?

In this hilarious game, your friends and family try to fool each other with your answers to questions like these in *You're Pulling My Leg! Junior.*

Winner of 7 Awards!

See more at MorningStarGames.com.

"The kids got a big kick out of this game and could not stop laughing."
- Parent to Parent

"Teaches while challenging children to understand what makes an interesting, compelling and believable story. Knowing your audience, playing to that audience and selling your ideas are some pretty heavy things to find in a simple game, but that is just what testers reported witnessing in their children as they played this game over and over. Along the way you'll be surprised how much you learn either about your own kids or about others."   *- The National Parenting Center*

"This is pure fun! We loved this game. It made us laugh hysterically. Encourages the players to interact and gives them a chance to learn about each other."   *- iParenting Media Awards*

OTHER GAMES FROM ALLEN WOLF

Discover the world of laugh-out-loud storymaking! Race against the timer to create stories using pictures, words, and a theme that change for each round.

You'll laugh hysterically when you hear the stories your friends and family crate. *JabberJot* will inspire your imagination!

Winner of 11 Awards!

See more at MorningStarGames.com.

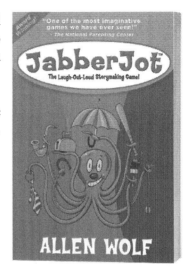

"One of the most imaginative games we have ever seen. Requires players to bring a sense of fun, silliness and creativity to the table. Perfect for large groups at a party, or for a quiet family game night with as few as four players, *JabberJot* keeps the action moving and the wild storylines flowing. You will laugh, groan and smile as you Jabber and Jot." *- The National Parenting Center*

"This game will help your child improve vocabulary and creative writing skills. Turn visual images and words into stories while engaging in endless imagination." *- Dr. Toy*

"This is a great party game. Fun and educational too." *- iParenting Media Awards*

OTHER GAMES FROM ALLEN WOLF

Pets have gone missing and it's up to you to find them! *Pet Detectives* puts kids and families on the path to finding their fun, furry friends in order to become the best pet detective in town.

Winner of 7 Awards! See more at MorningStarGames.com.

"Results in a completely entertaining evening that you can play with your kids. The names of the animal characters will launch peals of laughter." *- The National Parenting Center*

"It's entertaining and fun. Incorporates positive values and allows the whole family to play together." *- Dr. Toy*

"Our test family had a blast playing Pet Detectives. In fact, our young players wanted to play over and over again. Kids will love the adorable pictures of animals, and parents will love that their kids strengthen counting and memory skills." *- Parent Zone*

ALSO FROM ALLEN WOLF

Allen Wolf wrote the romantic dramedy novel *Hooked* that has won multiple awards and is now a major motion picture that is coming soon.

The novel is available wherever books are sold.

See more about the movie at HookedTheMovie.com.

"Wolf, an award-winning filmmaker, has adapted this first novel from his own original screenplay, and its cinematic potential clearly shows. The high-concept narrative is entertaining, well-paced, and highly visual. It's a charming, humorous, and hopeful tale. A quirky, touching love story that offers insights into autism, religion, and personal tragedy."

- Kirkus Reviews

"A wonderfully well-written, funny, romantic love story. Unique and inspirational. *Hooked* is not your average romance. Rarely do I find myself so captivated by a book that I cannot put it down for nearly two hours. *Hooked* is simply remarkable."

- Readers' Favorite

"Heartfelt, out-of-the-ordinary romance. This warm, witty story does not shy away from serious themes like exploitation, redemption, and true love. *Hooked* explores heavy issues with a light touch. It's easy to see this being adapted into an enjoyable movie."

- Foreword Reviews

ALSO FROM ALLEN WOLF

Allen Wolf wrote, directed and produced the psychological thriller, *In My Sleep*, which won multiple festival awards including *Best Picture* and the *Audience Award*. Watch now on Amazon, Tubi, or iTunes. See more at MorningStarPictures.com.

"Savvy Entertainment. Filmmaker Allen Wolf torques this high-concept premise to darkest dimension. Narratively, *In My Sleep* never rests, a credit to the tight, psychologically astute pacing of filmmaker Wolf."

- The Hollywood Reporter

"Genuinely suspenseful moments."

- New York Magazine

"*In My Sleep* is a brilliantly written thriller that genuinely keeps one guessing throughout the movie. The pacing is superb and the performances topnotch. Allen Wolf has created a very well made thriller."

- Movie Guide

SCORING SHEETS

SCORING SHEETS

SCORING SHEETS

SCORING SHEETS